Tell of His Wonderful Works

The wonderful things that the Lord has done for us

Georganne Stepp

I would like to dedicate this book to my wonderful husband Chris and my beautiful daughter Faith.

I would also like to dedicate it to my amazing parents, Elvin and Kathryn Smith, and my amazing in-laws, Rita Biffle and in memory of Johnny Biffle, and Ken and Robin Stepp.

Thank you all for your support, your prayers, and your love. You are each such a blessing in my life and a wonderful work of God!

Tell of His Wonderful Works

The wonderful things that the Lord has done for us

Advantage
BOOKS

Georganne Stepp

Tell of His Wonderful Works by Georganne Stepp
Copyright © 2021 by Georganne Stepp
All Rights Reserved.
ISBN: 978-1-59755-666-8
Published by: ADVANTAGE BOOKS™
www.advbookstore.com

This book and parts thereof may not be reproduced in any form, stored in a retrieval system or transmitted in any form by any means (electronic, mechanical, photocopy, recording or otherwise) without prior written permission of the author, except as provided by United States of America copyright law.

Unless otherwise indicated, Bible quotations are taken from the New International Version of the Bible. Copyright 1973, 1978, 1984 by International Bible Society.

Library of Congress Catalog Number: 2021950608

AUTHOR:	Stepp, Georganne
TITLE:	***Tell of His Wonderful Works*** by Georganne Stepp, Advantage Books
IDENTIFIERS:	ISBN: (print) 9781597556668
SUBJECT:	Inspirational

First Printing: February 2022
22 23 24 25 26 27. 10 9 8 7 6 5 4 3 2

Table of Contents

INTRODUCTION 7

1: HIS WONDERFUL WORK OF SALVATION 9

2: HIS WONDERFUL WORK OF MARRIAGE 17

3: HIS WONDERFUL WORK OF FAITH 23

4: HIS WONDERFUL WORK OF LIFE 29

5: HIS WONDERFUL WORK OF PROVISION 35

6: HIS WONDERFUL WORK OF GRACE AND MERCY 39

7: HIS WONDERFUL WORK OF ENJOYMENT 45

8: HIS WONDERFUL WORK IN ME 53

Georganne Stepp

Introduction

In Psalm 107:22, it says, "Let them sacrifice thank offerings and tell of His works with songs of joy." Revelation 12:11 tells us we can overcome the accuser of the brethren by the blood of the Lamb and the word of our testimony. Telling of all the wonderful things that the Lord has done is our testimony. It is powerful—powerful enough that with the connection of the blood of Jesus it can overcome evil. Thus, I felt led to start telling of His wonderful works in my life!

Thankfully, these wonderful works did not depend on me. The majority of these stories happened when I was the least "deserving of God's goodness" in my own eyes. Yet the reality is we are never deserving of God's goodness, even when we are at our best, because our best is like filthy rags apart from the righteousness of Christ, (Isaiah 64:6). That is why I am so thankful that God is a good Father and likes to give good gifts to His children, not because his children are good, but because He is good! So my hope and prayer is that these stories encourage you into a deeper relationship with Jesus, inspire you to worship Him more fervently, and most importantly spur you to tell of the wonderful works He has done in Your life. May God receive the glory!

Georganne Stepp

Chapter 1

His Wonderful Work of Salvation

Ephesians 2:8-9 "For it is by grace you have been saved, through faith-and this not from yourselves, it is the gift of God-not by works, so that no one can boast."

If I am going to tell of His wonderful works, it seems the best place to start is with His most wonderful work of all, salvation! I think it is important to note, this is His work, done for all who choose to believe in Jesus. So, I invite you to follow me if you will on my journey to His salvation work in me.

I grew up in a small church in Elizabethtown, Kentucky and I am very grateful for the experience I had there. I was baptized as a baby, and I am so thankful my parents made sure I had an opportunity to be at church every chance I could get. I went to church camp around the age of 12 or 13 and came back wanting to get baptized to confirm the decision that my parents made when I was a baby. I was very involved in the youth group. Also, in high school, I had a Sunday school teacher who started a small discipleship group. Through all these experiences, I became thankful for the way God was drawing me into a more intimate relationship with Him. For all practical purposes, I thought I had a rock-solid faith, then came college!

As with most college students who go away to college, my faith was tested. I am thankful I was still attending church with my grandparents, and I was a part of a Bible study through my sorority. I was still talking to God through prayer. I even remember a job I had at the mall where when times were slow, I would write letters to God. So that connection was still there, right? I mean I was still doing all the rights things, right? Yes and no. The actions were right, but some of the motives were wrong. Unknowingly, I was motivated more out of fear than love. Fear that if I did not do everything just right, I would lose my salvation.

Since I did not feel secure in my relationship with the Lord, this pushed me deep into the world, chasing after things that would not satisfy. Yet, on the other side I was still doing some of the "right things" and the connection with the Lord was still there, there was just something missing at a heart level. I did not realize that I thought I had to earn God's love and approval. I thought it was "my work" that was saving me, "my righteousness" that was making me holy or good enough to be saved. Thankfully, by God's grace, all that came crashing down one day on the campus at Western Kentucky University.

It happened one afternoon when I was at the Downing University Center, (DUC as we affectionately called it),

Chapter 1: His Wonderful Work of Salvation

and a girl with Campus Crusade for Christ came up to me and asked if she could ask me a question. I said sure; yet, little did I know that God would use that question to change the direction of my life forever.

She asked me if I were to die today, would I be 100% sure I was going to heaven. The question stopped me in my tracks. I had never had anyone ask me that question, or at least not in such a direct way. The beautiful part was, she was not condemning, or harsh, or scary. I truly felt love and compassion from her.

I answered her question something like "well, maybe, depending on how good I had been that day" (going through the mental checklist-like if I have not cursed that day, or been mean, or had any impure thoughts). Then, she went on to tell me that if I had been saved, I could be 100% sure I was going to heaven based on God's Word. She also shared some scriptures with me. I would love to tell you that at the moment I agreed that I could be 100% sure of my salvation and that I was going to heaven, but this began a journey over the next few years of discovering what His salvation work looks like.

The biggest part of the journey took place when I went to graduate school at the University of Kentucky. It was a time of rediscovering my identity and a lot of soul searching. I was stripped away from all that I had known the past four years, and everything upon which I had based my worth: friends, school performance, right behavior. I was in a marriage and family therapy program and we only had eight students in our group, so we became close very quickly.

Within our group, there was a variety of denominations within the Christian faith represented, and even a variety of other religions represented. This sparked something in me to really begin searching out who God was. I went to a variety of different churches, and even one that I think handled snakes, although thankfully we didn't do it that day! I had dear friends in the group that were of a totally different religion, and they took me to their place of worship. All the while, I had another dear friend in the group whose husband was in seminary, and they were praying for me not to convert to the other religion. It was like there was a war waging for my soul. I finally landed at a non-denominational church in Lexington, and once again God used someone to ask me an important question, and once again I was not prepared with a confident answer!

The scenario happened one day after church when I was sobbing (as I frequently did) wanting to grow closer to God, to really know Him, but not knowing how to get there beyond what I was already doing. This prompted me to meet with one of the associate pastors after the service, and he asked me a very simple question. He asked me if I was spending daily quiet time reading my Bible. I tried to think of a million different reasons why I wasn't, but none would suffice. The truth was, I simply wasn't.

His advice to me, which seemed so simple, yet so challenging, was to start by spending time in God's Word daily. You see, I loved praying to God, and I was probably reading a verse a day through different devotionals. While those things are wonderful, I had never really developed

Chapter 1: His Wonderful Work of Salvation

the discipline of reading God's Word in its full context on a daily basis, studying it, meditating on it, applying it in my daily life. While I thank God for prayer, I was spending way more time talking to God, than allowing Him to speak to me. I was like the seed that fell on shallow ground in the gospels. I loved the Lord, but I had no root. My faith had been based more on feelings than the truth of God's Word. Reading His Word would become my root and my pathway to know Christ more!

I remember I had a verse on the white board in my apartment in Lexington from Jeremiah 29:13, that said, "You will seek me and find me when you seek me with all your heart." I had not fully trusted God with my heart. So, I began "seeking" God more through His Word, and the eyes of my heart were open more to the fact that I was trying to earn His love and my salvation. Thankfully, I would eventually learn I did not have to earn His love and I could never earn my salvation.

Through this time, I also began to desire to be married, and I felt like God was calling me back to Bowling Green. I thought, "God, that is just a college town, I will never find a husband there!" Yet, I felt God calling me to trust Him. Not only would I find the relationship with Him I was looking for, I would also find my husband! So, when I finished graduate school, I moved home for a month, and then off to Bowling Green I went!

After visiting a couple of churches, I ended up at another non-denominational church. It was there that I really began to discover how much God loved me, and that I truly could not earn my salvation. A friend recommended the book, *"Search for Significance"* by Robert McGee, which is all about the fact that if we are looking for our identity in our performance, in people, in anything other than Christ, we will end up disappointed. Our significance can only come through knowing Christ. In the book there was that question again, "If you died today, would you be 100% sure you were going to heaven?" There was also a list of all these scriptures to support God's truth that we can be 100% sure. Thankfully, this time, God had prepared my heart to be more open to receive that truth.

Also, every week at church, I was hearing from scripture how we could never be good enough to earn our salvation, that is why Jesus had to die for us. I also learned that because of God's love for us, His salvation is a free gift from God when we place our faith in Jesus! So, by the grace of God, I finally accepted the truth and wanted to get baptized again because I finally got it! I finally opened the gift of God's work of salvation! And then to His next wonderful work, bringing me a husband!

Challenge:

As I mentioned in the introduction, my prayer is that each of these stories will spur you to share of His Wonderful Works in your life, so....

1. What is your story of His salvation work in you?

2. Please share your story with at least one other person.

3. Here are some scripture references that we can be 100% sure we are going to heaven if we have

Chapter 1: His Wonderful Work of Salvation

accepted His gift of salvation through faith in Jesus, and that it is not by our works: Ephesians 1:13-14, Ephesians 2:8-9, 2 Corinthians 1:21-22, Romans 10:9, Romans 3:20-28, Titus 3:4-7, and John 3:16

Georganne Stepp

Chapter 2

His Wonderful Work of Marriage

Genesis 2:22-24 "Then the Lord God made a woman from the rib he had taken out of the man, and he brought her to the man. The man said, 'This is now bone of my bones and flesh of my flesh; she shall be called 'woman,' for she was taken out of man.' For this reason, a man will leave his father and mother and be united to his wife, and they will become one flesh."

My journey to discover the husband God had for me was almost as interesting as the journey to discovering His work of salvation! Unfortunately, I was pretty "boy crazy" starting even in elementary school, always looking for the next boy to like! All the while, a very wonderful and God inspired experience happened in middle school in my youth group. Our youth leader passed out a poem called *"Wonderful Love"* at a lock-in at the church. The poem was very popular in the 1980's. The premise was that we cannot be satisfied with another person, until we are satisfied with God alone and the love He has for us. The poem goes on to talk about how God is preparing the person He has for us at the same time He is preparing us, so that we can both experience His "Wonderful Love" in the flesh. Sounds dreamy right! Well, I held on to this poem, believing that God did have somebody out there for me, someone that loved God as much as I did, if not more! And He did, it just took me a while to find him!

I would like to say after I got that poem, I quit liking boys altogether and prayed and waited on God, but unfortunately, I did not. You see, I have always had a bit of a rebellious streak that God has had to work out of me. So sadly, I turned to the desires of the world and looking for guys in all the wrong places, only to continually end up hurt and disappointed. Ironically, it was around the same time God was showing me who He was in my salvation journey, that He was showing me who He had for me. So, like I mentioned earlier, after I went to Lexington, God called me back to Bowling Green, to bring me into an authentic relationship with Him and a husband.

When I began attending the non-denominational church in Bowling Green, I also joined a small group called the twenty-somethings, because that is exactly what we were, a group of young adults in our twenties wanting to do life together. One night we were attending an outdoor worship event at a local venue and my friend and I were trying to recruit people for our group. We noticed a guy worshipping by himself that looked like he was in his twenties, so we went to introduce ourselves. Little did I know (until later) that right before that very moment, while he was worshipping, God told him to look down and

Chapter 2: His Wonderful Work of Marriage

to his right and there was his wife. Then, bam-I came up and introduced myself! And you guessed it, that guy became my husband. God is the ultimate matchmaker!

I would like to say that shortly after that moment we began dating, but in case you haven't gathered from my previous journey, I have a habit of doing things the hard way, my way! I had already started liking someone else in the group who was very nice, but I knew was not who God had for me. The other guy and I started dating, but thankfully God intervened! I began having dreams from God about my husband, and I knew I needed to break up with the person I was dating. Yet, even after breaking up, the first time Chris (my husband) asked me out, I said no. Poor guy!

I was scared of true commitment, scared of true love. Please remember I was also on this journey of learning what it meant for God to truly love me, warts and all, so it was hard for me to accept that another person could love me too. Yet, thankfully because of God's grace and patience with me, Chris asked me out again, and I said yes!

We started dating and through the dating process, we both realized we wanted to get baptized again. Chris wanted to because he felt he had done it for the wrong reasons, mainly for another girl he had dated previously. And as I mentioned in the last chapter, I wanted to get baptized because I finally received the true gift of His salvation. We decided we wanted to get baptized together. We scheduled it on my dad's birthday and invited family and friends. Excitement was in the air! Little did I know for more than one reason.

I lived in an apartment at the time, and sometimes Chris would pick me up to take me to church. The night before the baptism I had a dream that Chris was going to propose to me in the baptistry. Crazy right? When he came to pick me up, I told him about my crazy dream, and he just gave an awkward laugh. That should have clued me in, but I dismissed the dream and we went on our way to church.

One of our closest friends was up in the baptistry with us telling me he was there for emotional support, when actually he was a part of the surprise that was getting ready to take place! After we were both baptized, our pastor stepped back to the side, which was unusual since he would usually pray at that point. Chris stepped forward and motioned to our friend who was standing on the side of the baptistry back behind a wall where the congregants couldn't see. Our friend passed a paper to Chris, and when Chris began reading it, I couldn't believe my ears! It was the *"Wonderful Love"* poem. You see, I had made copies of that poem from my middle school youth pastor and I had passed it out to all the singles in the twenty something ministry. I never imagined it would now be read to me!

After reading it, Chris motioned again to our friend who passed him a box, and you guessed it, with a ring in it! I was already crying at this point, but then I lost it! I don't even remember Chris asking me, I just nodded yes through the tears of joy. And then our pastor loudly proclaimed, "She said yes!" It was a moment I will never forget of God's "Wonderful Love" displayed through baptism and my relationship with Chris.

Chapter 2: His Wonderful Work of Marriage

Challenge:

I truly believe there is an attack on marriage in our culture, so this is an opportunity for us to redeem what God has created! Marriage is His design and is meant to be used for His glory. It should represent to the best of our ability a picture of Christ, the bridegroom and the Church, His bride. Our marriage is not perfect, because we are imperfect people, but we have a perfect God, and it is His love for us and our love for Him that can empower us to love each other!

1. If you are married, what is your story of how you met?
2. Please tell your spouse all the wonderful things about him/her?
3. If you are single, are you finding yourself satisfied with His wonderful love?

Georganne Stepp

Chapter 3

His Wonderful Work of Faith

Romans 12:3 "For by the grace given me I say to every one of you: Do not think of yourself more highly than you ought, but rather with sober judgment, in accordance with the measure of faith God has given you."

After we were married, we continued to stay involved in church and I came to love different Bible studies. I was just soaking up the Word of God, but somewhere along the way I took a left turn in the pursuit of a "deeper level of faith." I was working pro-bono as a therapist for a family counseling center and a church was allowing us to use their space. One evening, I was talking to a well-meaning pastor from this church about issues with my thyroid. I had been taking medicine for my thyroid since I was 18 (I was about 29 or 30 at the time), and I believed God was slowly healing it, or at least reversing any damage because they had decided to reduce my medication after my last visit. Then the pastor asked me a question, but this one had a different effect on me than the last two questions. This one, without meaning to, left a sting of condemnation. He asked me what kept me from just quitting my medicine and having faith God would heal me. I thought, what is keeping me from doing that? I believe God can heal. He healed in the Bible, and He had already done miraculous things in my life, so why not this!

So that Sunday I prayed and asked God that if He wanted me to stop taking my medicine, He would give me a sign. And boy did He, but I did not realize until later it was to teach me an important lesson. Someone in the service had asked if she could stand up to testify, which never happened in our church because I go to a big church. Guess what she testified about? Being healed! Then, later in the service, our pastor stood on the edge of one of the chairs, which I never remember him doing before or since, and pointed to what seemed like me to ask if we believed God could heal. If that were not enough, the Bible study I went to that day was talking about one of the instances where Jesus healed someone. It was like God had a big megaphone saying, "Okay, big girl are you sure you want to pursue this level of what you think a 'deeper level of faith' looks like, then let's go!"

You see, even though I knew with all my heart that God could heal, I didn't have a peace in my heart that God's will was to heal me, at least not in the way I wanted to go about it! All I had in my heart at that point was fear and pride. I thought I was in charge of the healing, I thought I had to muster up enough faith, thus believing I had more faith than the next person. So, with that, I just stopped taking my thyroid medicine that I had been on for almost 12 years. I did not consult with my doctor because that

Chapter 3: His Wonderful Work of Faith

would have been a lack of faith, right? So sad to say, I had almost 4 months of misery.

Do you know what your thyroid does? A lot! My whole body swelled up, my feet, legs, even my face. I was exhausted beyond measure. My sleeping pattern was way off. And I thought I was emotional before, Hah! I never knew I could be on such an emotional roller coaster. I could not think clearly. Then I quit having my period. You would think all these would have been red flags, but in the name of faith, I kept pushing forward, not realizing I was in a state of complete denial. So much denial in fact, that when I quit having my period, I was convinced I was pregnant.

Therefore, I got a pregnancy test from the store, and when it came back negative, I assumed it must have been a mistake. Then, I made an appointment with my OB gyn and asked for a blood test. The blood test came back negative. Surely this had to be a mistake too! But the nurse insisted I start taking some medication they prescribed so I could start my period. I went home heartbroken and dismayed, still believing I was pregnant. I cried out to God saying I did not want to take anything that could harm a baby, and in God's great mercy, I started my period naturally the next day.

It was then I realized that I had to face the reality that God was not healing my thyroid, and that it was getting worse. I defeatedly called my doctor for a checkup. He wanted to get bloodwork done before my appointment. When it was time for my appointment, he did something he wouldn't typically do. He called me into his office. I must admit I felt like I was going to the principal's office, embarrassed and ashamed, but just like God in His character, my doctor's grace blew me away! He did not lecture me or scold me. He at first asked me if I had been taking my medicine, to which I simply responded no. Then I went on to explain my whole faith journey over the past few months, and he asked, "You don't go to a church that handles snakes, do you?" (Sound familiar from chapter 1!)

To which I said, "No, my pastor's wife is a nurse and she would definitely not condone this!" Then his response brought me back to the feet of Jesus, back to a state of humility. He said, "I do believe that God can heal, but right now science is telling us that your body is not healed and that you need this medicine. So, let's allow God to heal it naturally if He chooses, and the tests will confirm that."

I thank God for the lessons He taught me through this experience. I had come into an ugly place of pride, and I found myself comparing my faith to those around me, thinking mine was superior. I was working so hard to maintain my faith and try to make something happen, that it was still all dependent on me. You see, God did and does heal, and yes there are accounts in the Bible where a person's faith healed him/her; yet, let's look at the whole of scripture. The opening verse in Romans 12:3 says that the measure of faith we have is given to us by God! Even our faith is a work of God, that He gives to us and works through us.

I had also found myself in a place of discouragement, feeling I did not have enough faith because healing was not taking place. Yet, scripture also teaches that our

Chapter 3: His Wonderful Work of Faith

prayers of faith may not always be answered on this earth. Let's look at Hebrews 11, talking about the heroes of faith. In verse 13-16 it says "All these people were still living by faith when they died. They did not receive the things promised; they only saw them and welcomed them from a distance. And they admitted that they were aliens and strangers on earth. People who say such things show that they are looking for a country of their own. If they had been thinking of the country they had left, they would have had the opportunity to return. Instead, they were longing for a better country, a heavenly one. Therefore, God is not ashamed to be called their God, for he has prepared a city for them." This is so encouraging to know that our ultimate healing happens when we go to heaven!

So now I just try to rest in His work of faith, and there have been many times I have still slipped back into trying to have enough faith to make something happen, and it did not happen. Yet, I can honestly say there have been other times that **God** has given me a faith for something that I just knew that I knew that I knew, and it happened because it came straight from Him!

So yes, there is a "deeper level of faith" that His ways are not our ways and that if we abide in Him, He will give us the faith we need for the situations we face, and that His Will, will be done! Also, just a side note, after I got back on my medicine about 17 years ago, they had to almost double my dose, but over the past couple of years they began to slowly decrease it, so I thank God for His mercy and the healing that He has done! So on to the next wonderful work, the gift of life!

Challenge:

1. Has there been a time in your life where the faith you tried to muster up led to pride or discouragement?

2. When has God given you faith for something that you knew had to come from Him?

3. Please share these experiences with at least one other person!

Chapter 4

His Wonderful Work of Life

Psalm 139:13-14 "For you created my inmost being, you knit me together in my mother's womb. I praise you because I am fearfully and wonderfully made, your works are wonderful, I know that full well."

Shortly after my experience with the whole faith journey, and thinking I was pregnant, I had an amazing experience during my quiet time. I was reading in Genesis 18 when God was talking to Abraham about Sarah having a son even though they were both old and past the age of childbearing, and Sarah laughed. Then In verse 13-14 it says, "Then the Lord said to Abraham, 'Why did Sarah laugh and say, 'Will I really have a child, now that I am old?' Is anything too hard for the Lord? I will return to you at the appointed time next year and Sarah will have a son." I don't know if you have had those experiences where you feel like the words of scripture are talking directly to you. Well, that is what happened. These words just leapt off the page, and I felt like God was sharing a promise with me that I would either be pregnant or have a child sometime the next year. With everything that had happened, I did not want to become prideful or get back into "a work of faith." So, I just tucked it away, hoping I had heard God correctly and that I did not just make up what I wanted to hear, which believe me I have done so many times. That is why we have to confirm what we think God is telling us with scripture, with prayer, and with other believers. Then, we trust that if it is of God, it will happen. And thank you Lord, it did!

I became pregnant the next year and gave birth to our beautiful daughter, Faith Elaine Stepp, on March 1, 2006. She was and has continued to be such a blessing! One of the most beautiful things God has taught me through Faith is His unconditional love. While I knew at that point that my salvation did not depend on me, I was still struggling to believe that His love for me did not depend on me. Thankfully, in Romans 5:8 it says, "But God demonstrates His own love for us in this: While we were still sinners, Christ died for us." Also, 1 John 4:19 says, "We love because He first loved us." Therefore, His love does not depend on our perfect behavior, but He loves us simply because He is love and we are His creation! And oddly enough, God used Faith's quick desire to forgive at such a young age to teach me that she loved me simply because I was her mom!

I remember if Chris and I were in a fight, she would grab both of our hands (she was probably only three) to pray, or if I had gotten upset with her about something, she would be so quick to apologize and forgive my response. She so desperately wanted to restore the relationship. It was as if God was saying through her, "Look I love you

Chapter 4: His Wonderful Work of Life

just because you are mine and I want a relationship with you!" So, as I slowly began to realize that God loves me unconditionally, it allowed me to love Faith and Chris more unconditionally! None of us will ever be perfect on this earth, and this has freed us up as a family to love each other despite our imperfections. We have made our share of mistakes along the way, but in God's great mercy He has continued to redeem where we have messed up. Thus, it has been really special to see as a family of how God is growing us in grace and love, so we can extend that grace and love to others!

God has also used Faith in so many ways to teach us other things, including boldness, persistence, and courage, to name a few. This has brought to life one of the most fascinating things about God creating life, that He truly has a purpose for each one of us. If we pick up two verses later from our opening verse in Psalm 139, verse 16 says, "All the days ordained for me were written in your book before one of them came to be." So, if you would please permit me, I would love to share just one story of how one of Faith's ordained days came to be.

When Faith was in third grade, we were listening to Christian Family Radio and they were advertising about "Bring your Bible to school day," which is an annual day in October. Faith had asked if she could bring her Bible to school and reservedly, I told her we may have to check with her teacher. Well, thankfully Faith did not wait for me to check, and she took it upon herself to ask her teacher. Her teacher thought it was a great idea. In fact, her teacher suggested they start a Bible study at recess. So, they were having their Bible study at recess. Innocent enough, right? Well, next thing you know Faith and two of her friends were sharing the gospel with their other friends and asking them if they wanted to get saved. Now things were getting a little sticky!

Understandably so, her teacher said to respect everyone's beliefs, we would have to move the Bible study to before school and get parent permission. We understood and fully supported it. Gratefully her teacher continued to offer the Bible study the remainder of the school year. The following year, Faith had a new teacher and a new principal, so we had to start the process again. After attempts of trying to start it again and find a sponsor, the principal stated that technically to meet at school, it had to be a club, and to become a club, it had to be voted on by the Site Based Council. He was in support, but just wanted to make sure we were going through the proper channels. He also stated this would open the group to all the grades, where at this point it had just been for the grade Faith was in. While at first it seemed like a road block, we sensed God was up to something bigger, even bigger than we could imagine. (Ephesians 3:20).

While Faith and her friend got to work on a presentation for the Site Based Council of the benefits of having a Bible study group at school, one of Faith's friends from church said she had been inspired by Faith to start a Bible study group at her school. Her friend had approached one of her teachers to be a sponsor and their principal approved it as an FCA (Fellowship of Christian

Athletes) club! We asked their family to pray that ours would get approved too.

Then came the time for Faith and her friend to courageously present at the Site Based meeting. A vote was taken with a unanimous decision to allow the Bible study/prayer group to begin the following year, and it would also be listed as an FCA club. The principal stated this would open it up even more for guest speakers to come in from various churches and groups. Yet, it did not stop there! Through these two schools starting FCA clubs, more elementary schools began to join, and now there is one in several of the elementary schools in our county! Glory be to God!

Challenge:

So, as you can see, God created life for a purpose, so my challenge in this chapter is twofold:

1. If you have children, thank God for His wonderful work of life He has entrusted to you, and continue to pray and encourage them to fulfill the plan God has for them.

2. If you do or don't have children, thank God for your own life and continue to pray about the purpose He has for your life! It is never too late. As long as we have breath, God can and wants to use us!

Georganne Stepp

Chapter 5

His Wonderful Work of Provision

Philippians 4:19 "And my God will meet all of your needs according to His glorious riches in Christ Jesus."

As we all know, with a family comes needs, and thank you Lord He provides for all our needs, even when we don't know how. This became evident when our daughter was about two and a half. I was only working three days a week providing Christian counseling, while Faith was in a mom's day out program two days, and my mom would keep her the other day. Chris was working for an agency that helped young adults who had aged out of state custody to help them find employment and maintain stable housing. We knew his job was stressful and did not even seem to be a good fit, but we were not prepared for what was about to happen.

A few people had already lost their jobs at the agency where Chris was working. Then Chris came home from work one day stating that his boss had met with him, and that unfortunately his boss did not feel he was a good fit.

He stated that since he thought a lot of Chris, he would give him a month before the job was terminated to try to find another job. Well, I don't know if you have ever lost a job before, but this was a first for us. We were in shock and rattled, but thankfully God quickly gave us peace (notice I said God gave it to us, we did not muster it up on our own!) that surpasses all understanding that He would work everything out. I am so grateful for that "surpasses all understanding thing" (Philippians 4:7) because I definitely did not understand how He would work it all out, He just gave us peace that He would.

Chris started the process of applying for a new job, and we continued the process of praying. This was at the end of October, so we knew with the holidays around the corner, it may be possible that not many people would be hiring. In the meantime, Chris was volunteering with the junior high ministry at our church, and the junior high pastor had just randomly asked him how things were going, so Chris updated him and just asked for prayer. Then the unexpected happened. That Sunday at church, another pastor came up to us and stated that he had heard about our situation and wanted to help us with our house payment and electric bill for the next two months. We were shocked, humbled, and grateful all at the same time! God is so good! This gave us some breathing room while Chris looked for a job, and God, in His sovereignty, put me in the right place at the right time.

There was another therapist in the office where I was working who worked in private practice at our location and was also a center manager for a community

Chapter 5: His Wonderful Work of Provision

mental health center. Chris and I knew him well, as we went to church with him, and he and his wife had facilitated our pre-marital counseling. Chris had also worked for him at a different location when we first got married. Being a fellow Christian, I let him know what was going on so he could pray. Also, the community mental health center he worked for was one where Chris had applied, but in a different county; however, they had put a hiring freeze in place. Then to my amazement, he stated that the county where he was the center manager was hiring! Again, glory be to God! I shared the information with Chris, and he applied. He was offered the position by the end of the year, and he has been there ever since! But God's provision did not stop there, He provided a sweet Christmas surprise.

    A few days before Christmas, our doorbell rang. When we went to get it, there was no one there, but he/she left a huge bag tied at the top that felt as if it were filled with tons of goodies. Well Santa may leave gifts under the tree, but God left this gift on our front doorstep. We decided to wait until Christmas to open the bag, and through tears of joy, we lifted out so many amazing treasures. There were too many precious things to name, but just to name a few there was a beautiful hanging display with prayers on it that is still in our kitchen, a jar of delicious ingredients to make apple pie, and a beautiful doll house for Faith that she played with for years and we have kept to pass on one day. We have never found out who left the gifts that day, so we told Faith they were ultimately from God, echoing "Every good and perfect gift is from above," (James 1:17) and the "Father in heaven likes to give good gifts to His children." (Matthew 7:11).

Challenge:

1. How has God provided for your needs?
2. What "good gifts" has God given you?
3. Please share these stories with others!

Chapter 6

His Wonderful Work of Grace and Mercy

Nehemiah 9:31 "But in your great mercy you did not put an end to them or abandon them, for you are a gracious and merciful God."

Amazing grace, how sweet the sound. His mercies are new every morning. God's grace and mercy are truly amazing and they are weaved throughout the story of every believer's life. God's ultimate work of grace and mercy came through the death and resurrection of Jesus. If we look at a common definition of grace, giving us what we do not deserve, and mercy-not giving us what we do deserve, both were met through His death and resurrection. God gave us eternal life, which we did not deserve, and He rescued us from death, which we did deserve (Romans 6:23 "For the wages of sin is death"). Yet, God also demonstrates His grace and mercy to us on a daily basis, by giving us "good gifts" when we may deserve nothing, or bailing us out of our mistakes, when we deserve consequences.

Now please do not misunderstand me, we should not take either of these for granted, expecting God to give us good things when we have not earned it, or expecting God not to discipline us when we deserve it. In God's infinite wisdom, there are plenty of times that we either have natural consequences to our actions, or God steps in with loving discipline. In Hebrews 12:6 it says, "God disciplines those He loves," and this is for our good. Yet far more common is His grace and mercy in our daily mistakes!

While I could probably share a million times how His grace and mercy have been evident, I wanted to share one example that really exposed my own self righteousness and pride (These seem to be common themes with me, huh?), and that gave me a greater appreciation for His grace and mercy.

I was on my way one morning to take Faith to school, and she had to be there early that morning to put notes of encouragement in students' cubbies before they were going to have Star testing. I remember having a pretty confident attitude that morning because we had found out that Faith was going to be able to start the Bible Study back at school. Yet, later I realized that confidence was pride.

I was in the median to turn across traffic into the school. Then, a bus pulled into the median facing the opposite direction, so it blocked my view to ongoing traffic. I remembered looking right before it pulled in and I saw a car coming, so once that car passed, I was getting impatient and ashamedly had the thought "Well, God

Chapter 6: His Wonderful Work of Grace and Mercy

won't let anything happen to us, I mean Faith is going to be starting a Bible study." So, I blindly started across the two lanes of traffic to pull into the school. Then I remember seeing a car in my peripheral vision, and the next thing I knew, I was back in the median turned in the opposite direction. By God's grace, Faith was in the back seat on the driver's side, and we were hit on the front of the passenger's side. My heart was racing and I was in shock. One of the teachers pulled up next to me in the median and asked if I was okay. I said yes. Then, Faith's teacher was in the turning lane to come into the median and got out of her car and asked if we were okay. She said she would go on and take Faith to class if that was okay with me. I thanked her and said yes, I thought that would be the best thing.

Thankfully the other person did not have anyone with her, and she was okay. She did have pain in her leg, and I found out later she went to the doctor to get it checked out and was able to return to work the next week. The police came and of course, I took full responsibility. A tow truck brought me home and I just remember sitting in disbelief. Then Faith's teacher texted me to see if I was okay and would be able talk to Faith, so I called my neighbor and asked if she could please take me by school to check on Faith because Chris worked out of town. Thankfully she could, so I was able to go to school and talk to Faith and apologize profusely for being reckless and putting her in that situation. As usual, she demonstrated her uncanny ability to forgive quickly, and she accepted my apology and forgave me. Then, in a concerned voice, she asked if

I was going to have to go to jail. This lightened the mood, and allowed me a small smile and to be able to tell her no, thankfully I would not have to go to jail!

As my neighbor took me home, I was processing the situation with her not really knowing what we were going to do. We only had liability insurance on the car because it was older and had a lot of miles. She told me she had a family member who was a mechanic, and she would be happy to pass along his number to us. Then, after she dropped me off, I dropped to my knees crying out to God and His kindness led me to repentance. I realized that I had done exactly what Matthew 4:7 says not to do, I had put God to the test. I had done something reckless expecting God to protect me. So, I apologized and of course He had already forgiven me on the cross, but also in that moment. 1 John 1: 9 says "If we confess our sins, He is faithful and just and will forgive us our sins, and purify us from all unrighteousness." Thus, I experienced His great mercy, and then came His great grace.

That evening, Chris and I called our neighbor's uncle and he said he would come out and look at the car sometime the next week. Then we started to go into fix it mode, looking at cars online, trying to figure out a plan. Meanwhile, Chris and his dad had planned a father son trip for the weekend several weeks prior to this, to visit Chris's aunts and others family members who he had only seen a handful of times. Chris asked me if I wanted him to cancel the trip, but I knew God wanted him to go. Therefore, we did not cancel the trip and to our amazement God gave us a wonderful gift through Chris's dad.

Chapter 6: His Wonderful Work of Grace and Mercy

When his dad arrived from Atlanta, Chris was not home from work yet, so it was just Faith and me. When I let him in, he asked me to come outside because he wanted to tell me something. He then went on to say he wanted to give us his car and asked if I would be okay with that. He said he could rent a car back to Atlanta and get a new one there. I immediately starting crying, once again in awe of God's great grace and mercy, and graciously accepted the generous gift.

When Chris got back from his trip, our neighbor's uncle came out to look at the car and stated he would buy it from us and he would be able to fix it up, another huge blessing! God truly does do more than we can ask or imagine. Through all of this, I began to appreciate God's grace and mercy so much more, because in my pride and self-righteousness, I thought I had "earned" most of the grace and mercy I had received. Thus, when I made such a big mistake, I was humbled to learn that God had been showing me grace and mercy all along the way, regardless of whether I had "earned" it or not, but because He is a gracious and merciful God!

Challenge:

1. In addition to salvation, how has God demonstrated His grace and mercy to you?

2. How can you demonstrate grace and mercy to someone else?

Georganne Stepp

Chapter 7

His Wonderful Work of Enjoyment

> *1 Timothy 6:17 "Command those who are rich in this present world not to be arrogant nor to put their hope in wealth, which is so uncertain, but to put their hope in God, who richly provides us with everything for our enjoyment."*

This is such a wonderful verse. God not only provides for our physical needs, but He also provides us with things to enjoy! He wants us to enjoy things, and I am so grateful He has given our family so many things to enjoy. I am not necessarily talking about material things, which I am thankful for all that He has provided, but more specifically, I am referring to experiences that bring joy. The joy of the Lord is our strength (Nehemiah 8:10). So, I wanted to take the time to give God thanks and praise for a few of His wonderful works of enjoyment we have had the privilege to experience.

The first one came from an unexpected trip to Disney World. We had gone when Faith was in kindergarten to Magic Kingdom, and it was a magical experience except at the very end of the day, like at 10 that night! We all kind of had a family melt down when we were trying to find a place to stand to watch the nighttime fireworks and parade. Emotions were high and patience was small! It left a little sting, but we all eventually got over it, but who could imagine that 5 years later, when Faith was in fifth grade, God would offer an opportunity for redemption.

Faith was in the Beta Club at her school and they were preparing for the state competition. There are several different categories someone can compete in, so they were doing school competitions to see who would represent the Club at the state level. Faith had made it to the final round at the school level in a singing competition, so she and one other girl were selected to sing a song for the state competition. Faith had selected her own song when she competed at the school level, but this time the sponsor would select the song they would sing at the state competition. Faith said the sponsor had thrown out some ideas, and Faith did not know if we would approve or if she felt comfortable with the songs. It was not that the lyrics had cursing, but they were pop songs that just seemed a little too old for fifth grade, like one about someone being a cheater, and another about being obsessively in love with someone. Sadly, even if we would have been okay with hearing them, it seems to take a whole different meaning when you are the one singing them. Therefore, we all committed to praying about it.

Ironically, our pastor had just preached about Daniel not defiling himself in Babylon by eating the King's food. He explained that even though Daniel was going to be a

Chapter 7: His Wonderful Work of Enjoyment

part of the worldly culture, he had to set boundaries on what he participated in, and that we must do the same thing. It was as if God was preparing us that we may have to set a difficult boundary in this situation. I had also asked other people to pray and when I picked up Faith from the first practice, we had our answer. She was in tears, and said she felt convicted that she did not feel comfortable singing the songs they had selected. I had a good relationship with the sponsors and thought a lot of each of them, so I called one and explained that unfortunately we would have to graciously bow out of the singing competition. We did not want to ask them to change the songs. We just explained we did not feel comfortable with Faith doing it. She was very understanding and supportive and wanted to make sure Faith would be competing in something else. Thankfully, she had already tried out for the Quiz Bowl team and made that, so off to the state competition we went.

At the state competition, our quiz bowl team came in second place, and the first and second place winners qualified to go to Nationals that year, and guess where Nationals were? Disney World! We were so excited and grateful, and we felt God had blessed the difficult boundary we set. We did a few fundraisers to help offset the costs and were offered a group rate because of the Beta competition. This was an excellent deal and allowed us to visit all four of the parks. We had an amazing time! Also, to top it all off, we ended up at Magic Kingdom in the evening because of a weather issue. When we were getting off of a ride there, by God's grace we ended up walking right past the castle prior to the fireworks, so we practically had a front row seat to the show on the castle and the fireworks. It was truly magical and redemptive!

Another one of God's wonderful works of enjoyment involved Rock City and the Incline Railway in Tennessee. Every year, we take a trip to see Chris's dad and his wife in Atlanta, and the past few years, we have tried to do something on the way back. The summer after the trip to Disney World, we thought it would be fun to go to Rock City and do the Incline Railway. We had started talking about it at the beginning of the summer, but when it came closer to time, we had hit a really rough spot financially. I had moved out on my own in private practice, and my expenses were more than they were before. I had also had some issues with my checks from insurance payers not getting forwarded to my new address, and most importantly I had settled into complacency not wanting to work the number of hours in the summer I needed to cover the expenses, so it was a perfect storm!

We had drafted out a budget and figured that we needed about $100 to get into Rock City, ride the incline railway, and get food, but sadly we did not have $100 to spare that month. I felt so discouraged, and more importantly convicted that I had not been faithful with the time God had given me to work. I was too embarrassed to tell Faith, and I did not want to disappoint her since this was going to be our family vacation for the summer. So, I remember going back to my room and crying out to God and the thought came into my mind, "God, you can make water come from a rock, so I know you could make money come

Chapter 7: His Wonderful Work of Enjoyment

from nowhere." It was in reference to the scripture in Exodus 17 where God calls Moses to hit the rock so water can come out to quench the thirst of the people in the desert. Then, one of the most amazing experiences happened. As I was praying, Faith came running back to the room with a $100 bill and said, "Mom is this real? I found it in the tote in the living room?" I couldn't believe my eyes! It was real. Then, I vaguely remembered that we had gotten $100 from one of our parents for Christmas and I must have had it out on the arm of the chair, and it had fallen into the tote, to be found at the perfect moment!

Once again, God's wonderful work! We went to see Rock City and I saw one of the most beautiful scenes I have ever seen, water coming from a rock. It is the centerpiece of Rock City, this enormous rock with a beautiful waterfall flowing from it! It brought tears to my eyes and a smile to my heart. We took a family picture in front of it as a reminder of God's goodness and faithfulness!

Then on to one last wonderful work of enjoyment I would like to mention, our cat, Grace Kit! For a couple of years before getting our cat, Faith had been expressing her desire for a pet. We felt like we would not have the time needed to devote to a dog, so we thought a cat would be easier, but we were not totally sold on the idea. I had a dog growing up and I loved her dearly, but she stayed outside, so I had never had an indoor pet. Yet, Faith's persistence won my heart. The summer before we got Grace Kit, Faith had prepared an entire power point presentation on why we should get a cat. She had researched the cost, the benefits, and even agreed to pay for any expenses with her own money, and to clean out the litter box each day. Who can say no to that?

We told her we would think about it and pray about it. So as the holidays grew near, Chris and I decided we wanted to do this, but how? When? Then, the perfect opportunity came. She was in the Christmas play at church, so while she was at practice, we went to the Humane Society and filled out an application and began looking. While we were looking, a parent of someone who went to Faith's school was working there and asked us if we were considering adopting. We told her we were, but ideally, we wanted to try to surprise her for Christmas, so we did not know how to make that happen. I should have learned by now that I can't make anything happen, but God sure can! She told us that if we found one before Christmas that she would foster it for us, and we found out we lived on the same street, so she said we could even pick it up Christmas morning. God is just so amazing!

We did not find one that day, but we still had one more week before she would be out for Christmas break, so I went back to look a couple of days and we kept checking online. Finally, the Thursday before she would be out of school, I went back and the person I knew had sent me to another building. She sent word to give me special permission to go in the back to see some kittens they had just gotten in. When I went back to look at them excitedly, to my dismay they began hissing at me. The worker said she was sure with a little TLC that they would grow out of it. I wasn't so sure! I noticed in the cage below there was

Chapter 7: His Wonderful Work of Enjoyment

a tabby with some kittens, but she did not mention them. Therefore, I did not know if they were being considered for adoption, and I did not want to take advantage of the favor I had been shown. Thus, I left and told her I would be back in the morning.

I went home feeling discouraged and confused. It was just not quite how I thought it would go. Chris said maybe this was about more than just us finding a cat for Faith, but also rescuing a cat that needed to be rescued. I reluctantly tried to pray, but I just did not feel right about it; yet, I wanted to trust God. I went back the next day to tell them we would consider adopting one of the kittens. Then to my pleasant surprise, one of the managers asked if I was looking at the kittens in the top cage or the bottom. I told her the worker had shown me the ones in the top, and I didn't think the ones in the bottom were available yet. She then went on to explain that the worker did not realize that the ones in the top were feral, so they were not going to be put up for adoption, but the ones in the bottom were getting spayed and would be. I was so excited and said I would take one!

She told me their names, and there was one named Grace, so I knew that was the one! I couldn't believe this was really happening. Grace stayed at the Humane Society until they were closed for Christmas break, and the employee I knew fostered her for us. Then came that glorious Christmas morning, and Chris went down the street to get her. When he got back, Faith was still asleep, so Chris wanted to let Grace walk around a little bit to get acclimated. Well, there was no walking for her, she started running around the house, even jumping on the couch, which led to jumping right into our Christmas tree! Faith was still asleep, so we cracked her door and Grace walked in and we woke her up to her new bundle of fun and excitement! Faith affectionately gave her the middle name of Kit, and that is what we call her today. She never ceases to amaze us. She can walk on her hind legs, she sorted her toys into two piles when we were gone one day, and she plays fetch with her ball. She is truly a wonderful work of God's enjoyment!

Challenge

1. What wonderful work of God's enjoyment has He given you that you can thank Him for?
2. Please tell someone!

Chapter 8

His Wonderful Work in Me

Philippians 1:4-6 "In all my prayers for all of you, I always pray with joy because of your partnership in the gospel from the first day until now, being confident of this, that He who began a good work in you will carry it on to completion until the day of Christ Jesus."

Like this verse says, I am a work in progress, but I thank God that it is He who began this good work in me, and it is He who will complete it! So, my encouragement to you is that if you feel like you are a constant work in progress, it is because you are! Yet, you cannot complete it, only He can. So, what is our job? To abide in Him, to trust in Him, to follow Him, to spend time with Him in prayer and the Word, to delight in Him, to love Him, and to rest in Him!

Yet, I realize that for some of you, maybe this "work" has never started in you, because you have never received His free gift of salvation. This could be for a variety of different reasons. You may be like I was and think you had to earn your salvation, but the truth of God's word says, "There is no one righteous, not even one" (Romans 3:10), so we can never be good enough to earn our salvation. This takes the pressure off, realizing that we cannot earn it, but Jesus paid the price for us and offers salvation as a gift to us!

Or maybe you have thought you were a pretty good moral person, so that you never really thought about needing a savior, but "your good works" would be your ticket to heaven. And this is so easy for all of us to fall into, but God's word says that "All have sinned and fall short of the glory of God," (Romans 3:23) which means in comparison to a perfect, Holy God, we all fall short. None of us can be perfect. If we could have earned our own way, God would have never sent Jesus to die, but that is why Jesus says, "I am the way and the truth and the life. No one comes to the Father except through me," (John 14:6). But the good news is that this way is available to all who would believe!

Or maybe you always thought Christianity was about a list of dos and don'ts, instead of a personal relationship. Yet, my prayer through these stories is that you can see that God is a very personal God and wants a relationship with YOU! He wants to be involved in every area of your life. He created you and has a plan for you. He is madly in love with you, so in love with you that He sent His Son to die in your place.

You see, scripture teaches that we have all sinned, or done wrong things and these wrong things separate us from a perfect, Holy God. Scripture also teaches that the payment for our sin is death, so Jesus paid that payment for us by dying on the cross. This gave us the opportunity

Chapter 8: His Wonderful Work in Me

to no longer be separated from God but have a relationship with Him. And praise be to God, Jesus did not stay dead, but rose again, so we could live with Him forever! John 14:2 says, "In my Father's house are many rooms, if it were not so, I would have told you. And if I go and prepare a place for you, I will come back and take you to be with me that you may also be where I am."

So, for whatever reason you may not have received His free gift of salvation, it is my heartfelt prayer that you would consider receiving that free gift today. If you would like to receive that gift of salvation, the first step is to admit you have sinned and repent, which means to turn away from sin and turn to God for the forgiveness of your sins. Then, it is to ask Jesus to be the Lord of your life and live inside of you. Romans 10:9 says, "That if you confess with your mouth, 'Jesus is Lord,' and believe in your heart that God raised him from the dead, you will be saved."

So, if you would like to receive that gift, here is a prayer from Billy Graham to help you confess those words:

"Lord Jesus, I know that I am a sinner, and I ask for your forgiveness. I believe You died for my sins and rose from the dead. I turn from my sins and invite You to come into my heart and life. I want to trust and follow You as my Lord and Savior. Amen"

If you prayed that prayer, Luke 15:10 says that angels are rejoicing in heaven! This is just the beginning of His wonderful work in you. When we are saved, scripture teaches that the Holy Spirit comes to live in you (John 3:8, and 14:17), so we can never be separated from God because His Spirit lives in us! Scripture also teaches that when we are saved, we are born again, (John 3:3) so we start as "babies" in Christ and continue to grow and mature. He is with us each day, guiding us and working in us to look more like Him! So, if you did receive that gift, I encourage you to get connected to a local church to talk about baptism and how to grow in your relationship with Christ!

His work in us is a journey. It starts the day He saves us and is completed the day He takes us home. So, enjoy the journey and tell of His wonderful works along the way!

Georganne Stepp is available for interviews and personal appearances. For more information or requests email the publisher at: info@advbooks.com

To purchase additional copies of this book, visit our bookstore website at: www.advbookstore.com

"we bring dreams to life"™
www.advbookstore.com

www.ingramcontent.com/pod-product-compliance
Lightning Source LLC
Chambersburg PA
CBHW061514040426
42450CB00008B/1620